W9-BVD-609

Shazam

and Its Creators

INTERNET BIOGRAPHIES™

Shazam
and Its Creators

KRISTI HOLL

ROSEN
PUBLISHING®
New York

Published in 2015 by The Rosen Publishing Group, Inc.
29 East 21st Street, New York, NY 10010

Copyright © 2015 by The Rosen Publishing Group, Inc.

First Edition

Library of Congress Cataloging-in-Publication Data

Holl, Kristi.
Shazam and its creators/Kristi Holl.—First edition.
     pages cm.—(Internet biographies)
Includes bibliographical references and index.
ISBN 978-1-4777-7925-5 (library bound)
1. Shazam (Computer file: Music identification)—Juvenile literature.
2. Shazam (Firm: London, England)—Juvenile literature. 3. Internet
intertainment industry—Great Britain—Biography—Juvenile
literature. 4. Music and the Internet—Juvenile literature. I. Title.
ML74.4.S53H65 2015
006.5'40019—dc23

                                                    2014007972

Manufactured in the United States of America

Contents

INTRODUCTION

Shazam! This magic word was the name of an ancient wizard in the Captain Marvel comic books. Whenever the orphan Billy Batson shouted the word "Shazam!" he was transformed into Captain Marvel. From that beginning, the word "shazam" came to mean "magic" or "instant transformation."

Or, oddly enough, the name of an Internet company.

Suppose you hear a song on the radio, at a dance, or in a restaurant. You'd love to hear it again and even own it. If only you knew the name of that song! It's no problem anymore. Just Shazam the tune, and you'll have that information—and so much more—at your fingertips.

Using the Shazam app on your smartphone or tablet, hold the microphone toward the speakers that the song is playing from. From a small fragment of the sound track, Shazam will immediately show you the title of the song and the artist who sang it. You can then buy and download the song if you wish, or watch its music video. You can also download the lyrics for instant karaoke with your friends, or share music with friends on Facebook, Twitter, or Google+. During a big media event like the Super Bowl, the Shazam app lets

Shazam is recognizable today as a worldwide song-identification app.
Employees at the company's London headquarters monitor the service in
order to continually improve it.

you enter contests for free giveaways. Television commercials, brand names, and TV shows are also now "Shazamable," or able to be tagged. This helps viewers shop online instantly for items seen while viewing. This ability to provide instant gratification has helped Shazam skyrocket to the top of the business charts.

How is it possible to tag songs and brand names this way? Think of it like individual fingerprints. When you compare your fingerprint to others in a vast database, your fingerprint is immediately identifiable. It's the same with songs and other kinds of sounds as well, like the bark of a particular dog. Each has a unique "sound print" (or "acoustic fingerprint") that can be collected. When a person wants to quickly identify a certain song, the Shazam app helps users do this by simply listening to a very small part of it. It then screens its database of "sound prints" and quickly identifies the song.

By mid-2013, Shazam's music library held more than thirty million tracks. Shazam adds more than a million audio prints per month to its catalog. It acquires the tracks from music around the world. But that's not all. Shazam's team decided to focus on two key services:

"Name that tune" and "Buy that tune." They wanted users of their service not only to listen to the music, but also to cross over and become buyers as well.

Over time, the use of the Shazam music identification app became so widespread that Shazam's company name turned into a popular verb. You may have even heard it used that way. You may have wondered, "What's that song?" To which someone may reply, "Shazam it."

While the Shazam app is instant, there was nothing instant about the company's start-up. It took ten years for Shazam to transform into a billion-dollar business. The idea for this business was born in an unlikely place. It took the combined talents of four young men: Chris Barton, Philip Inghelbrecht, Dhiraj Mukherjee, and Avery Wang.

Together, they transformed a small invention into the magic of Shazam.

CHAPTER 1

The "Name That Tune" App

Hydrogen by itself is invisible and tasteless. Oxygen by itself is the same. But combine the two into H_2O and you have something totally new and amazing: water. While there wasn't a chemical reaction when the four company cofounders came together, something almost as magical happened. Shazam!

AN UNLIKELY BEGINNING

Cofounder Chris Barton was a student at the business school of the University of California at Berkeley. On the first day of his MBA classes in 1998, he sat next to Philip Inghelbrecht. They became teammates on a school project, developed a friendship, and decided to start a company together. They were brimming with ideas.

Barton and Inghelbrecht considered two other online business ideas before Shazam. One had to do with selling contact lenses on the web. Barton thought they could

Cofounder Chris Barton, who thought of the Shazam concept, first envisioned the music ID service when he was a business student in Berkeley, California.

make a lot of money with it. He called it a high-margin opportunity. Nonetheless, it sounded boring, and that idea was soon dropped. His friends jokingly called his second idea "e-stalker." It was an idea for applying "star power" to websites. For example, movie stars would allow themselves to be tracked online. Then, when you were on Amazon, for example, a pop-up might notify you that "Tom Cruise is on Amazon now." Barton thought websites would pay to have famous people tracked on their sites in order to draw more traffic. Later, he called it a crazy idea, too.

Barton was alone, trekking in the Himalayas in late 1999, when the idea for Shazam finally came to him. He dreamed of a service that would be able to identify hard-to-recognize music. His idea required two things: (1) inventing pattern recognition technology for creating acoustic fingerprints, and (2) forming a database of these acoustic fingerprints or "sound prints." Barton's original idea was to identify music by monitoring radio stations. He thought that he would sell the software to the radio stations themselves so that they could track their own programming and playlists. It would only work for songs featured on the radio.

As Barton was taking a business course called Strategic Innovation, he was encouraged to think much more outside the box. What if he could invent something so that a person could know what song was playing using the actual sound heard by a phone? No one had ever done that. So Barton called his dad, who was a nuclear physicist. While no expert in this area, his dad had a scientific mind and could help his son explore the idea. (Later, the company would be launched on Barton's dad's birthday, the nineteenth of August.)

Well, it was a great idea—Barton's brainchild—but Barton had no ability to invent the software and no business plan. So his next step was to find the people who could bring those skills and abilities to the company.

TEAMING UP

Barton's friend from UC Berkeley, Philip Inghelbrecht, was the second cofounder added to the Shazam team. In order to identify songs, the new company would need a giant database of musical "fingerprints." Inghelbrecht was the team member who took on that huge job, negotiating copyright licenses with people in the music industry.

Inghelbrecht admits that Shazam was a company that approached the business backward. Normally, a start-up company begins with the invention of a new technology. Only

Philip Inghelbrecht, the second cofounder of Shazam, was a friend and classmate of Barton's at UC Berkeley who would tackle the enormous job of establishing a database of songs.

then its market is identified, a business plan is designed, and money is made by selling it. Not Shazam. It had a company, an office, and people to run it before the invention of the technology. The founders needed someone who could invent what they wanted to sell: the ability to recognize a song simply by holding up your phone.

Before they found the person who would act as their engineer and inventor, however, Barton and Inghelbrecht added a third cofounder to the team: Dhiraj Mukherjee. He was the team member with the head for business, the one who made sure everything was in place when it needed to be, which would later include the task of raising funds. Oddly enough, Mukherjee had lived in San Francisco in the 1990s, and Barton had lived there, too. Then Mukherjee was in London in the summer of 1999 and Barton was there as well. They hung out and talked about starting a company together, but neither one had a specific idea in mind. Barton often mentioned his friend, Inghelbrecht, who was his classmate at business school. He wanted to involve Inghelbrecht in whatever he and Mukherjee would ultimately do together.

Mukherjee continued at his job in London, and Barton was back at business school in the United States when he came up with the idea for Shazam. At that time, in 1999, the most sophisticated things being done with cell phones were installing ringtones and sending text messages. Barton's idea for Shazam —using a cell phone to recognize music—was very much ahead of its time. Cell phones in the United States at that time had screens that consisted of two or three lines of black-and-white display. There was no way to show album art or play music samples.

Early cell phones lacked the features of smartphones. They could show two or three lines of letters and numbers, but they had no ability to show art or play music.

The cell phone market was much more advanced in Europe during that period. So it worked out well that Mukherjee was already based in London. For those reasons, Barton and Inghelbrecht finished business school in the United States and didn't take jobs after graduation. Instead, they moved to London. They didn't care much where they lived, as long as they had fun. This ability to move around—especially clear across the ocean to London—would figure heavily into Shazam's success.

TIME TO INVENT

Next the Shazam team literally went around the world looking for the person who could invent the technology they needed. They went to Xerox, the MIT Media Lab, and the Stanford University Center for Computer Research in Music and Acoustics—and most of the time they were laughed away. People told them that the invention they wanted was impossible and that there was no way to crack the code on music recognition in a noisy environment.

In spite of the opposition, they kept going. After extensive research on the web, they came up with forty possible names of inventors who could help them. They asked Julius Smith, a professor at Stanford, to rank the five smartest people on their list. At the top of the list was Avery Wang, who had done his Ph.D. in audio analysis at Stanford.

What made Wang stand out? He had the advanced scientific abilities they needed: acoustics signal processing, knowledge of math and statistics, and the ability to code and execute.

Chris Barton tried repeatedly to contact Wang, but Wang ignored Barton's e-mails. He had no idea who Barton was. Barton, however, wouldn't take no for an answer. Wang remembers Barton pressuring him to go to lunch with him at Café Brioche in Palo Alto, California (it later became one of their favorite places to eat). Wang thought the team was asking the impossible when they outlined their idea. However, Barton and Inghelbrecht were insistent that Wang could do it—and Wang agreed to try.

Barton and Inghelbrecht did extensive research hunting for someone smart enough to invent the app they had in mind. They found Avery Wang at Stanford University, where he had studied audio analysis.

Wang tossed around a number of ideas for several months but couldn't find a solution. Barton and Inghelbrecht got Wang some samples of songs recorded in locations where the average person might hear them. The recordings were poor, and he could hardly hear the music in the background. During the third and fourth months, Wang grew more worried. His cofounders were talking to investors, renting office space, and hiring people. But there was still no invention! Wang knew they had to have the software by a certain date. The pressure on him increased daily.

When did the breakthrough come? Avery Wang was doing what many creative geniuses do to find an answer. He was sitting in a café, relaxing, thinking, eating, and letting his mind wander. He was staring at some graphs when he suddenly realized that he had the solution right in front of him.

STRATEGY SESSIONS

While Barton was on vacation in Croatia for a week in 2000, two major things happened. Wang invented the technology they needed, and Mukherjee created a business plan for the company. In 2002, the team hired their new CEO, Jerry Roest, just a couple of weeks before the launch.

Mukherjee had another job at the time and was very busy. Still Roest asked Mukherjee to coordinate the business launch and to work out exactly what was needed to get underway. Mukherjee needed to make sure that all the different pieces of the business were in place: the music database, the mobile operator deals, and the actual working technology.

Mukherjee created a spreadsheet with every single task that needed to get done by the launch date. Every day as they counted down to the big day, Mukherjee walked around the office checking on progress. Piece by piece, tasks were crossed off the list. Mukherjee remembered very long work hours during that period. He would arrive at the office by 9:30 AM and work with the team until about 8 PM. After dinner, they'd all go back to work by 9 PM and work until about 3 AM. Even on Saturdays and Sundays, their team would work eight or ten hours a day.

Finally, one Friday, they had finished all the tasks and were ready to launch. However, Roest said businesses launched on Mondays were the most successful. So the date was moved, and Shazam launched the following Monday, August 19, 2002, which happened to be Chris Barton's dad's birthday.

The business didn't take off immediately. It would take the introduction of the smartphone and especially the iPhone for Shazam to truly succeed. Without smart-phones or the ability to identify and buy the music right away, the new business was slow. The Shazam app appeared three years before iTunes, seven years before the iPhone, and eight years before the Mac App Store. Some

Working the Shazam Magic

One reason for the phenomenal success of Shazam is the fact that all four cofounders were unique. They each brought something special—some set of skills, a particular personality, training, or work experience—that contributed to the blend that became the billion-dollar Internet business Shazam. The cofounders built off each other's strengths.

• Chris Barton is considered the creative genius behind the idea for Shazam. The idea for Shazam happened when he was hiking alone, and he understood how to coax his creativity out into the open. Barton left Shazam and joined Google about six months before Google went public, when it had only around two thousand employees. Nonetheless, he remained dedicated to Shazam through continued involvement as a Shazam board member.

• Philip Inghelbrecht was the lead person to build the Shazam music database and negotiate copyright licenses with the recording and music publishing industry. His friends said Inghelbrecht had incredible productivity, equivalent to the output of ten super humans. Inghelbrecht also eventually ended up working at Google. A few years later he went back into start-ups (including the websites TrueCar and RockMelt).

• Dhiraj Mukherjee was the team member who outlined the business plan and made sure all the pieces were in place when they needed to be. His middle name could be "Strategy." Mukherjee was responsible for fund-raising, managing the product, launching the service in the UK, and expanding into Europe. His cofounders appreciated how he always maintained such a calm attitude during some highly emotional and challenging times.

• Avery Wang was the principal inventor of Shazam's audio recognition algorithms and other key technologies. Without Wang, the company would have never gotten off the ground. At Shazam today, his responsibilities include innovation and intellectual property (patents). All four of the founders left the company at different points and for different reasons. However, Avery eventually rejoined Shazam and is still an employee today.

of the early employees even helped at Shazam for free (including a young student named Mekhala, who would marry Philip Inghelbrecht five years later). Between 2003 and 2004, Inghelbrecht worried that the company would fail. In fact, they had to lay off employees, including some friends, because they could no longer afford to pay them. There were some lean years, but when the iPhone did launch, Shazam was ready and waiting.

"I would strongly advise any entrepreneur not to try to follow this in any shape or form at all," Mukherjee said in an interview in *European Founders at Work*. "It's hard to imagine how one could set up a worse plan." In the beginning, Mukherjee had given the Shazam idea about a 4 percent chance of success. Even that was an overestimate, he admitted.

These early hardships meant that each success along the way meant a great deal to the whole group. Each time they hit a milestone in the company's development, they would all dye their hair. At different times, they had green hair, red hair, and blue hair!

A TEN-YEAR OVERNIGHT SUCCESS

Magic happened when the four cofounders came together, bringing their strengths and skills to a brand-new business idea. Shazam is still known as the "Name That Tune" app that identifies the titles of songs you can't remember or don't recognize, but it's come a long way since its beginnings in 2002. When the app was first introduced, users dialed 2580 (the four numbers down the center of a phone's keypad for easy remembering), and then held the phone near the source of the music playing. Shazam would identify the song, send a text message with the information, and charge a small fee to the user's credit card.

Today, Shazam identifies the song and so much more—much of it for free. There is no phone call to be made. With the Shazam app, users can "tag" a song (identify it), share it on social media, download it from iTunes, view it on YouTube, get the lyrics, and explore what's popular around the world with Shazam's interactive maps.

This company has been around longer than most Internet companies. Its slow growth and setbacks in the early years were both a challenge and a time of tremendous learning. The long, slow initial growth helped Shazam become a solid company, ready for the explosive growth that was to follow.

CHAPTER 2

Tag! You're It!

Imagine being in your favorite coffee shop or pizza place. It's noisy, but you hear a favorite song on the radio. You want to listen to it again. If it's an old favorite, you might want to download it. What do you do? With the free Shazam app on your phone, you "tag" it by holding your phone's microphone in the direction of the music. Instantly you get data about the song, a link to buy it, and a lot more.

How does the Shazam app work? Where can it be downloaded? How can somebody make the most out of the Shazam experience? While the invention is ingenious and complex, the app is incredibly simple and easy to use.

TAGGING MUSIC

The term "tagging" means marking something as your own. (It is similar to graffiti artists tagging and leaving their mark in public places.) With Shazam, tagging means marking music when a user hears something he or she likes on the radio, in a movie, in the mall, at a party, or anywhere else where there is music. The Shazam app marks the music somebody likes by taking a short sample and then identifying it for him or her. If a match is found, further information will show up on the artist, along with the song title and where to buy it, with links to programs or sites such as iTunes, YouTube, and Spotify.

A user doesn't need to remember the songs he or she tagged or the information provided. Shazam saves all tagged songs on its website so that each user has a record of everything he or she has tagged. A user might not have

Matching a song is just the beginning! Shazam gives additional information about the artist and where to purchase the song. Links take you to other sites, like iTunes and YouTube.

SHAZAM AND ITS CREATORS

the money to buy all the songs he or she tags, but since that information is saved, those purchases can be made later. It can be a great place to go with birthday and holiday gift cards.

How does tagging a song (marking it and saving it) work? When a cell phone's microphone is held up to the music, the Shazam app identifies what is known as the song's "numeric signature." This is as specific to music as a handwritten signature is to a person. Using a scientific formula patented by Shazam, the software analyzes patterns of frequency within the song. Then, the pattern is matched to a sample track in the Shazam database. Shazam can identify a song correctly despite background noise, even if the microphone captures less than 1 percent of the sound track.

We'll get into the science that makes tagging possible in a moment. But first, let's download the app onto your various mobile devices and begin to use it.

HOW TO USE SHAZAM

Shazam wasn't the first music app, but it took music apps in a whole new direction. There are several ways to use it, but one of the most convenient is to install the free app onto a cell phone. The Shazam app is versatile—it can be downloaded on a desktop, laptop, or tablet. The free version is available for such mobile devices as the iPhone, iPad, iPod, a Windows phone,

Getting started with Shazam couldn't be simpler! Choose and download the app for your specific device from the many choices on the Shazam website.

and BlackBerry. One big convenience is that Shazam automatically coordinates the songs tagged on all of a user's devices.

The first step is to download the app from the Shazam website (www.shazam.com). Simply choose the app for your specific device. Follow the instructions. Downloading is simple and quick.

Then you can begin using Shazam right away. Simply tap the Shazam button (or open Shazam on your computer) to activate the app. Many people leave the app running all the time so it's already on when a song is heard and can be tagged. The newest versions let the app run continually, tagging music automatically all the time, wherever you happen to be, and saving the information for you. This means users don't have to point and click anything—the app can now automatically do it all for them. The app makes use of the built-in microphone on either a phone or computer to scan any music playing in the vicinity and recognize the track from its audio "imprint" or fingerprint.

While it was expected that Shazam would be primarily downloaded to cell phones, many download it for their laptops and desktops. Countless people work on computers for long hours every day. They might want to identify a song being played over the office sound system. Or, while doing homework, others might want to identify their own music. Computers often hold sound tracks with file names

Want to identify songs already downloaded or ripped from CDs to your computer? Play them, and let your Shazam app identify them for you.

that simply read "Track 08" but don't include any specific song information at all. Should you play it or delete it? More information would be helpful. Shazam can give you key details as you play the song: the track name, the singer, the music composer, the album name, additional tracks from the album, a place to watch the track's video (or purchase it), and other information.

ENTER THE INVENTOR: THE SCIENCE BEHIND SHAZAM

We take apps for granted now, but stop a moment and think about Shazam's capabilities. What kind of brain can take an idea (like the music identification inspiration) and invent a process to make such a thing happen? To people who don't consider themselves creative, minds of inventors will always be an intriguing mystery. Avery Wang is the inventor and brains behind the science of the Shazam app.

Wang's idea centered on creating individual fingerprints for each song. But how do you "fingerprint" music? That was Wang's challenge. Fingerprinting music (or any sounds) relies on the use of a spectrogram. This is a visual representation on a graph of the spectrum (or range) of frequencies that exist in a particular sound.

Wang knew about trace and scatter plots when matching audio fingerprints. A scatter plot is a graph used to determine whether there is a relationship or connection between two distinct kinds of information. For example, such a graph might reveal a pattern when plotting variables like how far a golf ball travels when hit by clubs of various weights.

Wang got to work on the invention immediately. His Ph.D. studies at Stanford's Center for Computer Research in Music and Acoustics on auditory source separation

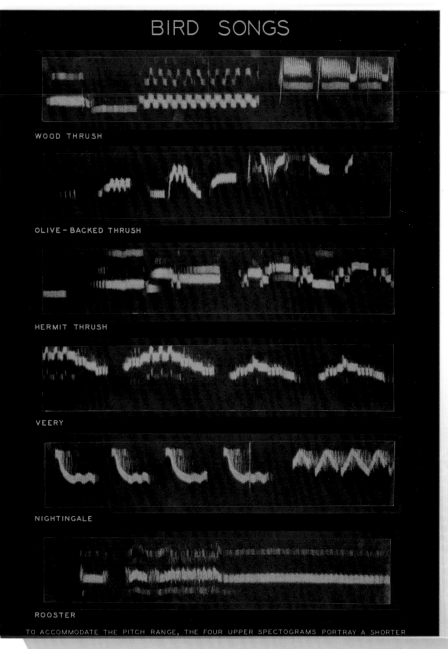

BIRD SONGS

WOOD THRUSH

OLIVE – BACKED THRUSH

HERMIT THRUSH

VEERY

NIGHTINGALE

ROOSTER

TO ACCOMMODATE THE PITCH RANGE, THE FOUR UPPER SPECTOGRAMS PORTRAY A SHORTER

A spectrogram is a visual representation of the frequencies of a specific sound. It is like a sound fingerprint. This graph depicts various sounds made by birds.

were put to use. Other scientists thought there was just too much information in a song to bring together a simple signature. But as he wrestled with the problem, Wang had a brilliant idea. What if he ignored nearly everything in a song and focused instead on just a few relatively "intense" moments? Intense moments might be very loud, very fast, or drop quickly from high volume to low volume. Most songs aren't filled with constant intense moments. They are scattered throughout the song.

Wang ran some examples and found that his solution was actually able to recognize music even in cases where the surroundings of the audio sample were very noisy. His invention created a spectrogram for each song in the Shazam database. Each spectrogram illustrates three elements of music plotted on a graph: amplitude (measure of change), frequency, and time. Wang's step-by-step procedure for calculating all this is called an algorithm. The algorithm picks out just those points that represent the peaks of the graph—musical notes that contain "higher energy content" than all the other notes around it.

Wang alone is credited with inventing the original Shazam app. Anybody interested in going deeper into the science behind his invention is in luck! Wang gives access to a document online that gives the full scientific formula with charts and graphs that explains his Shazam invention.

Over the years, Wang's responsibilities in the company have grown to include innovation (new advances)

The Way to Win

Without Wang's invention, the other cofounders would have had nothing to market. In a May 2012 interview on TheRecapp.com, Wang was asked, "What is the best advice you've received as an app developer?" Since Wang studied as a Fulbright Scholar in Germany and held a doctorate in electrical engineering—in addition to three other degrees in mathematics and electrical engineering from Stanford University—you might think the so-called best advice would be to get a good education. Not so.

Wang said the best advice was when he was told, "Given a choice between getting it out early and getting it right, get it right. Otherwise you will be killed." In other words, don't rush it. Releasing an app too early—one that doesn't work quite right—will kill the project. The new app won't be able to overcome the initial complaints and overall feeling that it was a dud. Getting the app right the first time is far better than having to apologize, fix it, and then convince the buying public that you have a new and improved version. As the saying goes, "You don't get a second chance to make a first impression."

and intellectual property (including copyrights and patents). By early 2014, according to the World Intellectual Property Organization, he has been granted seventeen patents.

BUILDING A DATABASE

Although Wang patented the ability to create audio fingerprints, that was only half the challenge. Yes, in theory, a tiny portion of a song could be identified when matched against a massive database of songs. It's similar to how law enforcement officials match a person's fingerprints against a database.

It sounds obvious, but they had no database. Just how was Shazam's music database to be built? The songs belonged to someone else, and after making the audio prints, who would own the rights to the songs' fingerprints? This was a very big question!

At the time that Shazam was ready for business, there were no musical databases that the founders could access. They had to start from scratch. This was at a time before digital music was widespread, when music existed primarily on CDs. In order to build an audio database, they needed access to thousands of CDs.

The cofounders hoped to avoid buying the one hundred thousand CDs that they would need at a cost of a couple million dollars. This is where Philip Inghelbrecht came in. He was able to arrange a phenomenal deal with

Entertainment UK, the biggest wholesale distributor of CDs in the United Kingdom. Entertainment UK had one hundred thousand unique CDs. If anybody had music in its warehouse, it was Entertainment UK. Shazam didn't need full digital copies of the music itself. Using Wang's technology to recognize music, it just needed enough to make a small audio fingerprint.

The deal Inghelbrecht arranged said that Entertainment UK would allow Shazam employees to move into its stores and pick CDs off the store shelves. Shazam would create its database using Entertainment UK's CDs.

Shazam hired a strict, ex-military man named Bart. His job was to manage the twenty-four-hours-a-day, seven-days-a-week operation that consisted of twenty young kids who were flipping CDs to extract the audio fingerprints. They also kept track of the song titles, album titles, track lengths, and other data.

But what would Entertainment UK get from the arrangement? At first glance, it sounds very one-sided. In return for using its CDs, Shazam let Entertainment UK keep a copy of the database for its own purposes, giving Entertainment UK valuable data to expand its online music sales. This deal saved both companies huge amounts of money.

Although an online file-sharing service called Napster was popular in late 2000, nearly everyone was still buying his or her music on CDs at that time. The iTunes store didn't exist yet; digital music was very new. Companies wanted to sell their CDs online, but the only way it could be done was if the CDs could be described. Before Inghelbrecht struck a deal, Entertainment UK didn't have the necessary digital information to use to sell CDs online. Afterwards, it did. It was a profitable trade-off for both parties.

Shazam's deal also helped the music industry itself in several ways. It helped spike sales, helped sell CDs online, and provided free publicity for the musical artists as well.

The Shazam cofounders had to build a music database from scratch. At that time, music existed in stacks of CDs at the local music stores.

TAKE YOUR PICK!

People want choices, and Shazam gives app users many options. According to Shazam's statistics, by July 2013, one in five iPhone users in America was using the Shazam app. By January 2014, fifteen million songs per day were being tagged or identified. What's the key behind such phenomenal success?

Most of it is the Shazam service itself. The product is clever as well as popular. It cuts out unrelated background noise, allowing users to name a musical score in a movie or television program, and even to identify a song played in a restaurant, mall, or the car.

Some of the success comes from Shazam's continually upgraded services. Shazam offers three different plans: a free version, Shazam Encore, and Shazam (RED). The free version, with unlimited tagging, gives music lovers plenty of features to enjoy. The only slight drawback is that the free version includes advertising that users may find annoying.

By late 2013, the following could be done on the free version of Shazam:

- Search, discover, and recognize music and songs.
- Buy tracks on Amazon MP3.
- Watch the videos for tagged songs on YouTube.

- See what other friends have "Shazamed."
- Use a service called LyricPlay to sing along to streamed lyrics like karaoke.
- Listen to the music you Shazam on the Rdio or Spotify online music services.
- Check out an artist's bio and discography (a full list of his or her recordings).
- Preview and save a list of favorite tags.
- Share music tagged in Shazam on Twitter, Facebook, and Google+.
- Shazam even when there is no network coverage; Shazam will match the tag when a connection is restored and come back with the result.
- Explore what's popular around the world with Shazam's interactive maps.
- Shazam from the home screen of a user's phone with the Shazam Widget.
- Play previews of tweets of users you are following right in Twitter through Shazam's Twitter Card.
- Explore more dynamic charts that show the most popular songs in the last seven days.
- Tag any TV show in the United States.

The paid Encore version of Shazam contains all the features above, but it takes out the distraction of the advertising. It also includes a few extra features including a Tag Chart, info on tours and live concerts, and videos. Shazam (RED) is identical to Encore, except that 20 percent of the purchase price is contributed to programs to fight HIV and AIDS in Africa.

Shazam is integrated with Facebook and is in a partnership with Spotify's music-streaming service to make it easy to purchase tagged music. Even more incredible features are continually being tested and released by Shazam, which will be discussed later. Shazam isn't just for music anymore.

CHAPTER 3

Small Start-up with Global Ambitions

The beginning of the Shazam story is not the moment the app was launched. The true Shazam story started more than twenty years earlier, when the four cofounders were young boys. In many ways they were just like any other children, and yet the spark of genius was planted early.

WHERE DID IT ALL START?

For Chris Barton, his relationship with his father was very important. His father was a professor of nuclear physics and an entrepreneur himself. He came from a poor background and was raised by a single mom during the World War II and postwar eras. He was an expert in neutron radiography and developed N-rays (similar to X-rays but with the ability to see through metal). He took N-ray radiographs of air force jet wings that were susceptible to water corrosion inside. His mother also played a key part in his future interests. When

Chris was eleven years old, his mother brought home a Sinclair computer, and Chris taught himself how to write simple software programs on it.

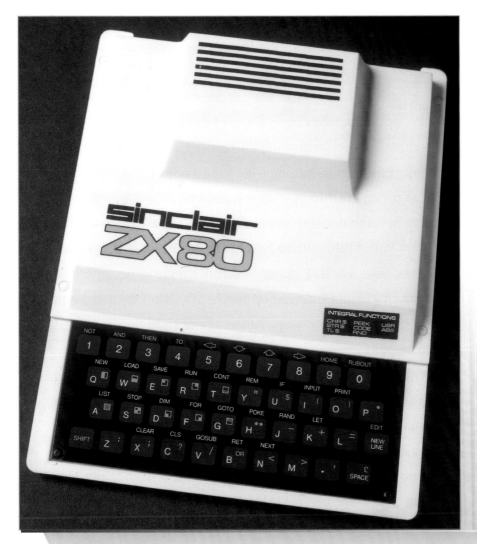

As with many inventors and entrepreneurs, Barton's home environment impacted him greatly. When he was only eleven, he wrote software programs on a Sinclair computer his mother had given him.

Dhiraj Mukherjee was born in Delhi, India, but he grew up all over the world. His father was an airline manager, so his family moved often. Growing up, he lived in Athens, Paris, Calcutta, Geneva, and Bombay (now Mumbai). When he was thirteen, his family bought him a ZX Spectrum computer. His family wasn't wealthy, and the computer was a big expense, but it shaped Dhiraj's life and interests. He learned to program in the programming language called BASIC and wrote simple video games in his bedroom after school. He credits his mother, a musician, for his love of languages. His grandfather, who was an admiral of the Indian navy, taught Dhiraj focus, determination, and an unwavering belief in doing the right thing.

Philip Inghelbrecht got his first computer at age fourteen, and he also began writing simple programs. His parents taught him the importance of working hard and earning his own money. At the age of eight, Philip got his first paid job—selling Christmas trees. His dad paid him twenty-five cents to help people pick out a tree and trim a few branches. However, he didn't tell his dad that most customers were tipping him a dollar. Philip worked from that time on, including some not-so-glamorous cleaning jobs. He names his parents, who have been constantly supportive, as the biggest influence in his life.

Avery Wang had very tolerant parents. He traces his interest in technology back to the first grade, when he saw an episode of *Star Trek* in which Captain Kirk (who was fighting a monster known as Lizard Man) figured out how to make gunpowder from ingredients he found just lying around. The recipe was given in the show, so Avery wanted to try it. His parents let him create the explosive, and Avery was hooked on doing science experiments. He once built a device for making prank phone calls. Avery says he was never good at mental arithmetic, but he did well with abstract topics. He taught himself calculus in high school and only had to show up to take the tests.

Each of the four cofounders brought childhood skills and characteristics with them to the Shazam table.

THE DIAL "2580" APP

The first Shazam app was popularly known as "2580." It required users to first dial "2580" on their cell phones and then hold up the phone to the music. The music picked up on the call was analyzed for an audio fingerprint and then run through the Shazam database. The results were sent to the user in a text message, and the user was charged for the text. Today, Shazam users can hardly imagine using such an old-fashioned system to identify a song. Now Shazam can instantly identify music—as well as TV shows and products. Shazam has come a long, long way!

When the service first launched in 2002, it was known as "2580" because those numbers went down the center of the phone keypad. Most customers would use the app out of curiosity three or four times, but then stop. The Shazam

The Shazam music ID service was first known as "2580," an easy-to-remember number that goes right down the middle of every phone's keypad.

smartphone app was launched in 2008 at the same time that Apple's App Store launched, positioning itself as one of the first apps available for iPhone users.

Both the growth of iTunes and the huge success of the iPhone's App Store fed Shazam's growth. The use of apps simply exploded. According to former Shazam CEO Andrew Fisher, originally people might have fifty apps on their phones but would only discover three. Suddenly, with the huge success of the App Store, there were eighty-five thousand apps available in one place. The average consumer was downloading eight apps just in the first week. By late 2009, over ten million phones had downloaded the Shazam app.

Growth has been phenomenal. Fifteen years after the initial "2580" idea was birthed, Shazam could be found on most major platforms, such as iOS, Android, Windows, Windows Phone, and BlackBerry.

FROM THE SILICON VALLEY TO THE UK

An area south of San Francisco, California, has been called Silicon Valley because it is known for its huge number of computer companies. Three of the four cofounders once lived in this area of the United States, and yet Shazam was launched in the United Kingdom. With most of the team living in the United States near the birthplace of many other tech start-ups, why move clear across the ocean to launch their new service in London?

The main reason for the move to England—and why there was more interest there—had to do with technology. In 2000, cell phone service across the United States was unpredictable. You couldn't even send a short text message (or SMS) across the country yet. Calls frequently got broken up and sometimes didn't get through at all. The whole Shazam business model was built on the idea of being able to send short text messages back to the user (while charging a fee for it). The U.S. cell phone market simply wasn't set up yet to handle that.

Also, the per capita music market (or the average amount of music bought per person) in the United Kingdom was higher than anywhere else in the world. People in the United Kingdom were listening to more music, so there was a potential for more users of the Shazam app. Those in the United Kingdom had been using cell phones

Chris Barton (*above*) and Philip Inghelbrecht moved from California to London, England. People in Great Britain bought more music, and cell phones were being more successfully used there. Both factors were critical to Shazam's success.

(which Europeans call "mobile phones" or "mobiles") with greater success for a number of years already. Because of that, they were more open to the idea that the Shazam app could actually work.

Not all four cofounders relocated to London. Avery Wang, the inventor, already had a family and preferred to remain living in Palo Alto, California. Being an inventor, Wang's best ideas were as likely to be generated at three o'clock in the morning as during regular business hours, so his presence wasn't actually required in the London office. However, Barton and Inghelbrecht relocated to London, where Mukherjee already had a job.

Shazam's first office was Mukherjee's apartment, since the founders were on a very limited budget. At that time, they had no outside funding at all, so every expense was paid for out of the founders' pockets. In the summer of 2000, they had enough funding to get their first real office, a tiny eight-foot-by-six-foot room in a dingy building in the heart of the Soho neighborhood, which was the media region of London. Later, when a company closed its offices, they were able to take over its London office space, furniture and all. It was in a fantastic location on the edge of Soho near Piccadilly Circus, a popular public plaza.

The cofounders had a great idea. They had the invention ready and the patent for it. They had the time. They had the enthusiasm. But they were missing one major item: the money.

Piccadilly Circus lies at the intersection of five main roads in London's West End. It's a large open space surrounded by several major tourist attractions, including theaters and stores.

SHOW ME THE MONEY

Finding money for their new business was the most challenging goal the founders faced in London. They also had to win the support from cell phone companies that hesitated to partner with Shazam. Shazam was a brand-new business, unheard of, that could go belly up overnight. Before agreeing to work with Shazam, phone companies needed to see that its idea was backed by important business people: investors.

Investors are people who believe that a company can succeed—and they believe it strongly enough to invest their money. New start-up companies (like Shazam was at the time) have no history yet of financial success, so they can't get traditional bank business loans. Instead they need two kinds of investors. The first type is called the "angel investor." Angel investors are often successful individuals who believe in the new idea so much that they willingly put down personal money to help make it happen.

How could these young men persuade investors to contribute to their new business that was really just an unproved idea at that point? Wang built a demo to show possible backers. He played a little audio clip recorded over a cell phone. The clip would be compared against the database of songs, and the software would then identify that song. His demo would look very out of date today, but at the time, it looked like magic. The demo plus a PowerPoint presentation sold the investors. The original PowerPoint presentation painted a picture of a service that would some day enable people to do things such as buy the music, watch music videos, see lyrics, send music greeting cards to friends, find out which songs their friends were tagging, and organize their favorite music into playlists. Many of those features took years to create but ultimately became possible after smartphones were common.

It's a Small, Small World: Going Global

Shazam has grown from that small start-up company based in one London office to now having global headquarters in London and New York, plus offices in Menlo Park, California; Los Angeles, California; Chicago, Illinois; and Seoul, South Korea. The Shazam app is being used in many foreign countries because Shazam's database includes thousands of songs in native languages. Shazam expanded into Latin America in 2013, as well as Canada, Australia, Brazil, Mexico, and India, among other countries.

Around the world, the numbers tell the story:

- Shazam is available in thirty-three languages in two hundred countries.

- It has over 350 million users, adding about 10 million new users a month.

- In September 2013, five hundred thousand songs a day were sold through Shazam, which equates to around 10 percent of the digital music sold around the world.

- Shazam landed $40 million from Carlos Slim (América Móvil) to develop its TV advertising business and grow in Latin America.

- Shazam expanded Rdio integration beyond the United States, landing in Canada, the United Kingdom, Australia, Brazil, and Mexico.

- Shazam landed a partnership with Indian music streaming service Saavn.

- Shazam opened an Australian office as the music ID service targeted TV ads across Asia-Pacific.

The cofounders chose to raise angel money from investors who were already famous. When a well-known wealthy person invested in them, it gave other investors more confidence to put their money into the brand-new company. Shazam's famous angel investors included the founder of Amazon.co.uk (Amazon's U.K. website), the former chairman of BMG (a major record label), and the former chief tech officer of British Telecom, a telecommunications company. Those names attracted a lot of attention, helping the founders raise a total of $1 million in angel money.

Then it was time to move on to the second type of investors: VCs, or venture capitalists, who are sources of larger amounts of money. While angel investors contribute their own personal money, venture capitalists belong to firms that use other people's money to buy shares in private companies like Shazam. Venture capitalists take great risks, so they usually receive some control over company decisions and part ownership in exchange for their investment. Venture capitalists look for a strong management team, a large potential market, a unique product or service, and a company ahead of its competition. The young Shazam company had all of these qualities. By July 2001, the cofounders had raised $7.5 million from venture capitalists.

BEWARE THE COMPETITION

While Shazam clearly leads the pack in the music identification business, a number of services are in competition and would like to give Shazam a run for its money. Building a successful company is something like a race. You must look ahead to see where you're going, but you also must glance back to see if competitors are gaining on you.

Here are some of Shazam's competitors—and what they offer that is different.

- SoundHound: This phone app for music identification doesn't require a song being played for the ID. A person can just sing or even hum a tune, and it will let the user know the name of the song in only a few seconds.
- Tunatic: Tunatic is a song identification system for Windows computers only. It requires a computer with a

Shazam has been able to win over more users than its competitors in the music industry. Only by knowing what competitors are doing can a business stay ahead of the game.

microphone. Once it finds a match, it will list the title of the song and the artist's name.

• Audiggle: This free app for your computer identifies music that is playing on your PC (in a movie, on a live-streaming TV show, or from an Internet radio station). Audiggle limits your free searches to five per month. For more than that, you need its paid service.

• musiXmatch: musiXmatch is primarily a lyrics app with a music ID feature built in. Tests in 2013 showed Shazam correctly identifying nearly twice as many songs as musiXmatch.

• Rdio: In January 2014, Rdio eliminated the time limit on its free music streaming service where you can listen to songs for free through its U.S. website.

• MusicID: It has many of the same features as Shazam, but there is no free version of the app.

• Beats Music: From the moment you first open the app, Beats starts logging your "music DNA." This serves as a personal profile used to determine which albums and tracks you might enjoy the most. Beats Music makes suggestions for other albums and songs you might like to listen to and buy.

• Spotify: In January 2014, Spotify removed all time restrictions on its music streaming service. Users can now listen to their favorite songs as many times as they like, for as long as they want. (For a small fee, subscribers can listen to a catalog of more than twenty million songs.)

Shazam was not an overnight success. It traveled many miles from its beginnings as a new invention in California to become a billion-dollar, global business with headquarters around the world. As we will see, Shazam has moved even beyond song recognition into multimedia, while maintaining its same high standards in the music business.

This branching out has kept Shazam well in the forefront of this business, and the future couldn't look brighter.

CHAPTER 4

Trials and Tribulations

Persistence is the key in any business getting off the ground because there are always expected—as well as unexpected—obstacles at first. Shazam has successfully overcome many challenges.

CONVINCING PHONE COMPANIES

In the beginning, inventing the app software was a huge advancement, but the challenges were far from over. Before Shazam could sell its music recognition service to the general public, the founders had to convince cell phone manufacturers to carry it. Could these companies be persuaded to see the value of Shazam and be willing to distribute the service on their phones?

That was the next challenge. A large number of meetings with cell phone carriers came next. If Shazam failed there, it would all be over. Cell phone carriers competed with each other for customers. Shazam assured them that a fun-to-use

Shazam convinced cell phone carriers that phones could be used for more than talking to friends. In fact, Shazam's music ID service could be a fun selling point.

music recognition service installed on the phones would be a big selling point—that cell phones could be used for more than just chatting with people or leaving a message.

In order to do this, however, Shazam needed two very specific and different things from the cell phone carriers. First, it needed a special, lower SMS (text message) rate, like those that many other companies were given. The initial Shazam app would send the text message to the user with the name of the song; the user would also receive a charge on his or her phone bill. Shazam wanted a share of that phone bill charge. Its profits depended on it.

The second thing the Shazam team wanted was not common at all. In fact, it took many months to convince the phone companies to go along with the idea. What was the "new thing" that Shazam wanted? A short, four-digit phone number, something easy for users to remember (like calling 911 for emergencies). The number the team wanted for Shazam was 2580, the four digits that go right down the middle of the phone's keypad. The founders had to convince each different phone company to give them the same 2580 number to avoid confusion.

Eventually, after much persuasion, cell phone manufacturers and carriers saw the value of Shazam and were willing to give the service a try. By then, other trends were more favorable, too. Cell phone companies had started selling ringtones, and they realized they could make extra money with special services such as Shazam.

The cofounders had overcome some huge hurdles by this point: getting both the invention and the database of signatures, raising money, getting the 2580 phone number they wanted, persuading phone companies to carry them, and dealing with layoffs.

The early years were filled with tough times. How did the founders get through them as a team? According to an interview in *Mad Men of Mobile*, Barton said there had never been a fallout among the cofounders. Barton thought it definitely helped that they started as friends. It was during the low points, he said, that their friendships kept them together.

SHAZAM CUSTOMERS SMOLDER

While millions of users were very happy with how the Shazam app worked for them, not everyone was delighted. Since 2004, Shazam has constantly upgraded and improved its music identifying service. Sometimes after an upgrade, however, the service stopped working correctly for some users. In 2012, there was a high rate of online complaints about Shazam.

Here are a few of the many complaints taken from the Bad App Reviews website:

- "I've used this app since it was first released—their poor customer support has caused me to switch to Sound Hound."
- "Fix it, guys, I paid for this app."

- "Tons of us have been having connection problems for months with no response."
- "Don't waste your money. Support is a joke. They won't respond. Taking money and not providing a working product is ridiculous."
- "Shazam used to be a great application, but now it rarely works. Won't even support paid version."
- "Connection errors and still no response from support with two open tickets. Purchased app and want refund as it seems they don't care about fixing it or communicating with customers."

The complaints fall under the headings of "poor customer service" and "poor technical support." Customer service boosts the level of customer satisfaction after a purchase, and it includes troubleshooting any problems a customer may encounter. Technical support services, or tech support, attempt to help the user solve specific problems with a product. Tech support may be delivered over the telephone or online by e-mail, live support on a website, or a tool where users can log a call (sometimes called logging an incident or a ticket).

Good customer service is vital to the success of any business. A business can gain new customers by offering promotions and slashing prices. However, unless customers keep using the service, a business won't make money for long. Today, with more music recognition services available, unhappy users can move to one of Shazam's competitors with just a couple of clicks.

Since such a high percentage of people are using the free service, should Shazam bother worrying about their complaints? Yes, because complaints give a company valuable information about what needs to be fixed, and good customer service means keeping customers happy. Happy customers write good reviews, make word-of-mouth recommendations to their friends, and pay for upgrades. To keep them happy, tech support must respond to complaints and questions in a timely manner. If a website promises a response within twenty-four hours, there needs to be follow-through within twenty-four hours. Reliability is vital.

Shazam's complaints dropped off significantly when its customer service and tech support improved.

PARENTAL CONCERN ABOUT SHAZAM SERVICES

The Shazam website has a "protection of minors" notice that says people must be of age thirteen or older to use the app. Additionally, if you are under eighteen, you must have a parent or guardian's permission. You'll only find this warning if you search long enough for it. There is no link to this warning from the "terms and conditions" anywhere on Shazam's main landing page or product pages.

Do people read this warning? Maybe—if they can find it. When you locate the web page, the warning is embedded partway down a very long page of solid print.

Why the age warning and parental concern? Some concerns include explicit song lyrics and products that children find when clicking links to third-party websites.

Explicit Lyrics: Despite Shazam's age warning, children under thirteen are using it. Many have Shazam access on phones belonging to parents, older siblings, or friends. They use Shazam like anyone else, to find songs, hear the words, watch videos, and read the lyrics. Kids from

The Shazam service is intended for users aged thirteen or older. Users aged thirteen through seventeen must have the permission of a parent or guardian because of access to explicit song lyrics.

ages six to eleven have posted reviews of Shazam at the Common Sense Media website. One review (by an eleven-year-old) was entitled, "What parents need to know." The child's review, marked for offensive and explicit language, said, "Parents need to know that ... song names and lyrics can contain iffy language with mature references. Kids can post music information through a direct connection with Facebook or Twitter." Another review by a different eleven-year-old said: "I love this app but...there is a downside. Sometimes you may not realize it but the song your [sic] listening to may be uncensored and on Shazam the lyrics contain explicit language." (Nowhere on the review site was there any mention that Shazam is not intended for kids under thirteen.)

Third-Party Websites: Parents also worry because the Shazam app links the user to third-party websites. Some of these websites are for adults, with content and products not necessarily appropriate for children. Some third-party websites may also record a child's location. Shazam's difficult-to-find policy page does cover that:

"Shazam may enable you to use ... Third-Party Sites and Applications ... (including social networking sites, sites on which you can view content and from which you can make purchases, or record a geographic location that you find yourself in) ... We are not responsible for and have no control over any third party content, advertisements, links ..."

Red Band Trailers

Another concern for parents is a feature called Shazam for Red Band. Shazam has teamed up with movie production companies for a new twist. When watching television and a caption appears at the bottom of the screen that says "Shazam for Red Band," it means you can launch your Shazam app on your phone or laptop to see a Red Band trailer. A Red Band trailer is an "age-seventeen-and-up" graphic movie trailer that most parents don't want their children watching. Movie theaters do not allow them because of their graphic sex, violence, language, and drug use. The "Red Band" name comes from the color that comes on the screen before the trailer. (Trailers acceptable for general viewing are green.) Parents worry that children and young teens with access to the Shazam app will be exposed to the graphic content of Red Band trailers.

GREED, DEBT, AND INSTANT GRATIFICATION

Shazam makes it possible for people of all ages to instantly purchase music and a variety of products while watching Shazamable TV shows and commercials. There is concern that Shazam services feed consumer greed and encourage undisciplined instant gratification. With consumer debt already out of control, does Shazam add to the problem? Some parents feel that Shazam's "buy now, think later" policy is really a "buy now, regret it later" policy. Time to calmly consider a purchase is snatched away by shopping with Shazam. By the time a consumer thinks about his or her decision, the music has already been downloaded or other purchase made.

Yes, because of the Internet, it is very easy to shop now. A person watching the commercials—either live or videotaped—can see something he wants and tap the Shazam button on his smartphone or tablet. The consumer will then be taken directly to the stores selling that product, be shown his choices, and be able to buy immediately. The whole process will be finished—and his credit card will be charged—before the commercial ends.

This could be called convenience, and it certainly saves time. But does it also encourage undisciplined instant gratification? Some people think so. The "I want it right now" itch is immediately scratched. Instant gratification bypasses the once common series of actions: working, saving money, working some more, saving some more, shopping around for good deals and sales, then buying the item when you can pay for it in full. That would be called delayed gratification, which helps develop patience and keeps a person out of debt.

Shazamable TV shows, instant downloads, impulse buying—it's all certainly convenient. But there can be a

Shazam makes instant online shopping easy. You can buy songs, albums, and products associated with a sound track. Convenience? Or an instant way to dig yourself into debt?

downside to all this convenience. The ease of buying on cell phones and mobile devices may be spurring users on to buy more. Sometimes they buy more than they need. And often they buy more than they can truly afford.

LAWSUITS AND LEGAL PROBLEMS

After a number of years, businesses that become successful have occasional legal problems. Lawsuits may get filed in hopes that the successful company will pay out some money to drop the suit. Other people truly believe that they have a grievance to settle, and they want the courts to make it right. Shazam has had a number of legal issues come up over the years, including:

- Tune Hunter Patent Infringement Case: In May 2009, Texas-based Tune Hunter sued Shazam Entertainment (along with ten other companies) over alleged patent infringement. Tune Hunter claimed it filed the patent back in 2005, and it was a very similar music identification system. Shazam was the first defendant to settle Tune Hunter's claims.
- Digimarc Patent Infringement Suit: In November 2009, Digimarc Corporation filed a lawsuit over patent infringement against Shazam Entertainment. In June 2010, in Beaverton, Oregon, Digimarc dismissed its complaint. Instead, Digimarc and Shazam discussed ways to work together.
- Blue Spike Patent Infringement Complaint: On August 9, 2012, Blue Spike, LLC, filed an infringement complaint in Texas against Shazam Entertainment. This is a claim for patent infringement. As of early 2014, no judge had yet been assigned to the case.

At any given time around the world, different people can be working on the same invention, totally unaware of anyone else working on it. When a company is built around an invention, it is to be expected that some disagreements over patents will arise. It is one of the trials and tribulations of being in business.

BUMPS IN THE ROAD: ADVICE FROM THE COFOUNDERS

The beginning of a start-up isn't the only time that trouble can occur. Each stage of business brings different challenges. Initially, problems center on designing a superior product and raising money from investors so that a company can go forward with its production or service. Later, marketing and customer relations are bigger challenges. Furthermore, businesses continually deal with the ups and downs of the economy, over which they have no control. All these challenges require perseverance and creativity, plus the ability for cofounders to work together.

How did the Shazam cofounders deal with such challenges? What advice were they given—and what advice would they pass along?

Barton has warned other entrepreneurs that building a start-up is a whole life experience. Since there is statistically a much higher chance that a business will fail than succeed, there need to be additional benefits to starting one (such as learning, excitement, or spending time with friends). And what's the key to entrepreneurial success? "Persistence," Barton said in an interview in *Mad Men of Mobile*. "If you are not prepared to go to superhuman levels that are beyond rationality to realize your dream, then your chance of finding success is virtually zero."

Mukherjee's advice was to find balance between determination and having fun. Both are very important. From his grandfather, Mukherjee learned that if you put your mind to something and decided it had to be done, you would succeed. His grandfather did not allow doubt or hesitation or fear, and Mukherjee tried to imitate that determination.

But life was not meant to be grim, he cautions in an interview in *Mad Men of Mobile*. "As long as you are having fun, you will make good decisions, manage stress, not take things too much to heart, and remember that there are more important things in life than a business: true friends and family who will support you regardless of your success or failure."

CHAPTER 5

Second-Screen Media Engagement

In more recent years, Shazam's technology has expanded beyond song identification to other media. A January 2011 study conducted by Nielsen and Yahoo! found that 86 percent of mobile Internet users (and 92 percent of thirteen- to twenty-four-year-olds) were using their mobile devices simultaneously with television. A quarter of them said they were browsing content related to what they were watching.

In order to take advantage of this trend, Shazam started applying its technology to television ads and shows, making them "Shazamable." That meant Shazam would do the online searches for the viewer and deliver the information through its app. All nationwide television shows in the United States have now been Shazam-enabled. Wang's audio imprint technology has been used to team up with other companies, brands, and mega-events. It appears to be the way of the future.

THE SECOND-SCREEN EXPERIENCE

Shazam can now identify video content by use of a sound print, and this has enabled it to extend its influence into second-screen experiences. The "second screen" is the tablet or smartphone in the viewer's hands, turned on and ready, while he or she watches something on the television (the "first screen"). A large percentage of viewers were watching the television with a second screen open in their hands or on their laps. They were texting, posting about a show on Facebook, or Googling a movie star's name for additional

Viewers watch TV shows while using a tablet, smartphone, or computer to text friends, post something on Facebook, or use Google to obtain more information about shows and product brands.

information. That's where Shazam stepped in as it teamed up with various product brands and TV shows.

Shazam wanted to train viewers to start Shazaming commercials and TV shows as much as music. Television advertising reaches an amazing number of people, but the level of involvement with a TV commercial is small. In fact, most people tend to ignore ads, mute them, or take the time to raid the fridge. The challenge for Shazam was to change the viewer's thinking about commercials.

A December 2013 study reported on Informilo.com said that 45 percent of those being polled claimed they used wireless devices to do research while watching television, while 41 percent used the devices for impulse buys. (Those in the study were not necessarily Shazam app users.) Another 2013 report on TechRadar.com showed that nearly 85 percent of Shazam users used the app for a "second screen experience" with either a TV commercial or a TV show. That was good news for Shazam! Why? Because it had developed technology to simplify the user's experience—and help the sponsors sell more products. Using Wang's technology, a connection to a commercial could come through any kind of audio fingerprint at all, whether it be a song or a bouncing basketball or the sound of a soda can being popped open.

When using the app with a TV show, Shazam users can call up a programming guide on their second screen, read information about the show and cast, buy music from the show, read celebrity gossip and trivia, and then share it all on Facebook, Twitter, and Google+. The TV feature exists within the Shazam app, and this TV tagging eliminates the search engine, bringing content directly from the TV screen to the viewer's second screen. Users stay engaged with the show, even after it is over. It also transforms them from passive viewers into active customers.

In 2014, Shazam found ways to keep the viewer "attached" to the products long after the show ended. For example, if someone tagged a TV commercial about a Jaguar car and shared it on Facebook, in the weeks and months after the show, that user would be "retargeted"

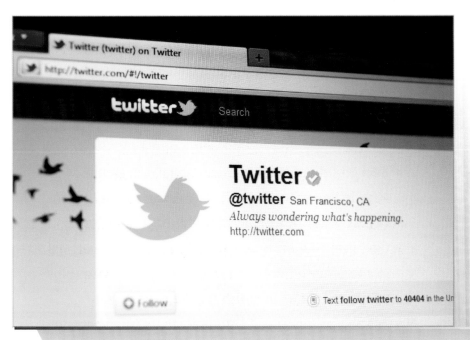

Shazam users can "tag" a TV show and use their second screen to read about the show and cast. They can instantly share celebrity news on Twitter, Facebook, and Google+.

with advertising about Jaguars. Tagging the commercial with Shazam marked those users as more likely to buy a Jaguar (or whatever product was tagged), so they were added to a targeted customer list.

TV TAGGING

When you see the Shazam sign or logo while watching a TV show, just tag it and pull up extra content tailored to that specific show. Shazam can even leave be left running in the background all the time, continuously tagging music, TV shows, and commercials and saving the tags for later. Do you like the running shoes the star is wearing? Shazam them and a link will appear taking you directly to an online store where you can purchase them. Extra content is almost instantaneous in its delivery.

What kind of information might you expect if you Shazam a TV show?

- Background music and theme songs: Shazam uses its huge inventory of over twenty million tracks to identify the music featured in TV shows.
- Cast information: The app will list the cast featured in the program, any guest stars who appeared, plus additional shows in which they've been.
- Trivia: Fans can read little-known details about the show, plus view bloopers and outtakes that didn't appear on the show.

Look for the Shazam logo in the corner of your TV screen and tag what you are watching. Extra content about your favorite show will be delivered to you immediately.

- Celebrity gossip: The app gives fans all the latest talk about the celebrities in the show.
- Social networking: Fans talk with their friends about what they watch by commenting on Facebook or replying to the live Twitter feed.
- Web links: For even more information, fans can click on links to show-related websites on the Internet, including the official site for the show.

The free TV-tagging app works with a variety of devices including iPhone, Android, Windows Phone, BlackBerry, Nokia, iPod touch, iPad, and any computer running Windows 8.

Shazam moved from being just a music-discovery company to becoming a media-engagement company by the end of 2013. In a short period of time, the television business became a major source of income for Shazam. David Jones, the executive vice president of marketing, claimed that television business would soon be Shazam's primary source of revenue. Despite Shazam being enormously successful and long lasting, the company knows that it must change as technology and the world changes. If Shazam had stayed with its original service of dialing in a request and paying for a text message response, it would have gone out of business many years ago. To remain successful, it had to stay alert to how the world was changing and evolve along with it.

Daniel Danker, chief product officer for Shazam, summed it up well in a TechRadar.com interview: "When you are reaching more than seventy million users a month you have got an incredible platform....We are scaling up what we are doing on music, then using our technology to build a business in television." Judging by the results so far, Shazam is well on its way.

BRANDING: NOT JUST FOR CATTLE ANYMORE

Brands of clothing, cars, and snack foods are teaming up with Shazam so that a particular sound or song is tied to each brand. Then that audio fingerprint, when tagged by the Shazam app, brings up all kinds of information on the user's second screen. The audio fingerprint might be a snippet of a song track, or it might just be a sound like squealing tires or the crunch of potato chips. Then, when a viewer Shazams the product on the big screen, the app identifies the sound print and the product to which it is attached.

Using the Shazam TV app eliminates use of a search engine. Shazam brings products seen on the TV screen directly to the viewer by way of the "second screen." Both Shazam and the makers of the products share in the money generated by this app. It is an inventive way to keep viewers who use the Shazam app connected beyond the end of the thirty-second commercial spots. It also transforms them into buyers on their second screens—their smartphones and tablets.

Shazam for TV enables more than one hundred million users in the United States to tap the Shazam app button, and in a few seconds, be introduced to a second-screen promotion built specifically for the brand. More than 300 television ad campaigns from over 150 famous brands—such as Pepsi, Toyota, and Sony Pictures—are using Shazam for TV to instantly provide more information, special offers, and the ability to shop directly from the couch. What could be easier?

BEYOND TRADITIONAL COMMERCIALS

Most people view commercials as something to suffer through in order to watch the show. Shazam sees the advertising differently. In November 2013, a campaign for the Jaguar F-Type showed how the app could extend an advertiser's influence. When viewers who were interested in the car Shazamed a thirty-second commercial showing the exterior of the car whizzing by, they were then taken to a three-minute tour of the car's interior on their hand-held mobile device or notebook.

Viewers won't be bombarded with extra things that don't interest them, but they will be offered additional information on the things they do want. People

Second-Screen Social Network

In March 2013, Shazam partnered with Facebook so that each service could gain functionality from the other. Shazam users with a Facebook account could now easily compare songs with their Facebook friends, discussing what they were listening to and buying. They could also display their tagged songs on their Facebook walls.

A map also displays the most popular songs being listened to around the world. Users can then click over to hear the song on YouTube or get the lyrics through LyricsPlay. LyricsPlay, an interactive aspect of Shazam, makes it easy for karaoke fans by highlighting each line of a song.

And what about TV shows? Shazam has tapped into today's active social networking for that, too. Shazam users can now automatically share those tagged TV ads and products with friends on Twitter, Facebook, and Google+. Shazam app users can discuss what they like, the pros and cons of the products, and more. And it's all from the comfort of the living room couch!

wouldn't Shazam an ad for something they don't want. People Shazaming ads generally want to know more. Why would someone Shazam a shampoo commercial, for example? She might get access to styling tips. When a Shazam user sees the "S" icon flash on a TV ad with a suggestion to use the app for some extra content, he or she may receive anything from a song to a coupon. Over the last few years, Shazam has come to play a big role in advertising, making TV ads interactive in some of the world's biggest televised events.

CROWD PLEASERS

It makes sense. The fastest way to make big sales via Shazam is through second-screen engagement where crowds are gigantic. Shazam has delivered advertising at such mega events as *Britain's Got Talent*, the Grammy Awards, the Olympics, and the Super Bowl.

While the 2010 Super Bowl had the first Shazamable commercial, it was the 2012 Super Bowl that paid off in "record engagement" by way of "millions of tags," Shazam's press release said after the event. It was the first major television event where Shazam enabled users to interact throughout the experience: some of the commercials, the game, and the halftime show. When thousands of users clicked on their Shazam app, they had a chance to win prizes, get free merchandise, participate in polls, unlock a free video, and and win a gift card—or even a car!

The 2012 Super Bowl between the New England Patriots and the New York Giants was also super for Shazam. Users interacted millions of times to win merchandise and gift cards.

The 2012 Super Bowl was a huge step up for Shazam, who partnered with almost half of the Super Bowl's forty-six advertisers. These Shazam-enabled partners gave away nearly one million prizes during the Super Bowl. By the 2014 Super Bowl game, Shazam was partnering with 100 percent of the advertisers.

In the 2012 Super Bowl, Shazam linked to commercials by Acura, Best Buy, Disney, FedEx, GE, Honda, Pepsi, Teleflora, Toyota, and others to unlock special content and coupons only for Shazam app users. Shazam

Super Bowl Confusion

Even though the Super Bowl of 2012 was a super success for Shazam, the numbers could have been higher. During the Super Bowl, many viewers were left in the dark about what they were supposed to do with the Shazam logo in the ads.

The intent was for viewers to fire up the Shazam app on their mobile phones in order to recognize the audio in the ad, which then would take them to giveaways and other additional content. Unfortunately, there were no clear instructions for viewers ahead of time.

With many ads running for only thirty seconds, it was impossible for many viewers to see the logo, pull out their mobile phone, start the app, and tag the audio in time to get the link to the free offers. It worked only for those who had their phones already on and the Shazam app running when the commercial started. It worked for those who were prepared, but not for the others.

The Shazam news feed feature has gone a long way to fixing this issue. App users are now notified before a big event about some freebies that will be theirs if they watch—with their Shazam app running and ready!

users could enter a Toyota sweepstakes for a new Camry; Best Buy gave away $50 gift cards; and Pepsi offered viewers a free video.

Was Super Bowl 2013 even bigger and better? Not exactly. In fact, after Super Bowl 2013, online analysts called Shazam a "niche player," or a small competitor. Research by Altimeter Group said Shazam's "brand adoption rate" actually decreased notably in 2013. (The brand adoption rate is how long it takes after hearing about a product or service before the public adopts it and uses it.)

However, with a new strategy, Shazam came back strong at the 2014 Super Bowl. First Shazam used its news feed feature to reach more than ten million users, reminding them ahead of time to tune in during the game to obtain exclusive free downloads. For example, when people Shazamed the Bruno Mars half-time performance, they received exclusive access to a video of his performance from a tour in Paris. For the first time, Shazam was connected to every commercial, making it easy for users to watch their favorite commercials (including those from 2013) over and over—and share them on social media.

Other mega sports events that are now Shazam-enabled include the Olympics. The 2012 Summer Olympics in London found Shazam in partnership with NBC, which included NBC Sports Network, MSNBC, Bravo, and CNBC. During the seventeen-day period, U.S. viewers Shazamed the Olympics several million times to get second-screen

Viewers of the 2014 Grammy Awards in Los Angeles Shazamed the show 70 percent more than in the previous year. Shazam notified millions of users ahead of time to tune in for free content.

extras, such as video clips, athlete stories, match results, and medal counts.

The 2014 Grammy Awards were also an outstanding success. Shazam users were ready. Using its news feed before the show, Shazam notified ten million iOS and Android users to tune in to the show for exclusive (and free) content. Viewers of the Grammys Shazamed more than 1.1 million times, a 70 percent increase over the 2013 broadcast. More than fifty-four thousand of them went on to purchase music by artists featured in the program.

CHAPTER 6

Shazam! Explosive Growth and the Future

Like any new company, Shazam had to overcome many setbacks and survive some big bumps in the road. It took Shazam ten years to surpass its first billion transactions. It took another ten months for the second billion. Later, it took only two months for the app to go from the ninth to the tenth billion. Shazam's last few years have shown even more tremendously accelerated growth. In January 2014, Shazam had 350 million users and was adding 10 million users a month. It had 180 people working for the company, most of them in London.

HITTING HYPER SPEED

Many, many Internet companies spring up overnight and often disappear just as quickly. But Shazam has lasted more than ten years—a long time for an Internet company—and it shows every sign of being here for the long haul. The four cofounders appear to have set up a very solid business.

What are the secrets to its success?

One thing has been its innovation—like using the audio fingerprints for TV tagging and branding. However, Shazam hasn't overlooked further advances with its music app as well. For example, it now allows auto-tagging. Even when a user doesn't specifically open the Shazam app, it can automatically run in the background while a mobile device or computer is on. Why is this handy? Perhaps you're in a meeting in a restaurant or just visiting with friends over lunch. In the background you hear a song, but it's rude to whip out your smartphone to Shazam the

Stay focused on your friends! Let Shazam run in the background, tag all the music played during your lunch, and keep a record for you. Check out the song list later.

song right then. No problem. Shazam can automatically run in the background, tagging all the music that plays while you're at your meeting or just while walking in the mall. Shazam keeps a record. You can go back later when you have time and see the songs that were played. If there was a particular song you wanted, just click the link and download it.

Although only one cofounder remains as a full-time employee of Shazam, the company has remained solid. Avery Wang did leave the company for a few years at one point, but he eventually returned. Wang is still working to fine-tune his recognition algorithm in order to implement new Shazam features and applications. While he still often does the code development himself, he does enjoy having a small research team now (instead of being the entire research department himself). Another of his responsibilities has to do with Shazam's patents and protecting its inventions.

MINDSHARE

The term "mind share" relates generally to minds sharing the same opinion, or using advertising to make certain brands the most popular in the minds of the customers. When people think of examples of a product—shoes, cars, colas, or search engines, for example—only a few brand names usually come to mind. "Mind share" tries to establish a certain brand (such as

Adidas, Ford, Pepsi, or Google) as being one of the best kinds of a given product or service. Sometimes brand names are so well known that that they become a synonym for the product or service. Kleenex, for example, is a brand of facial tissue. However, it became so well known that consumers often use the term to identify any tissue at all, even a competing brand. The same thing has happened to the word "smartphone." That's mind share to the max! For many people, Shazam has become that type of service. Want to know a song title? Just Shazam it!

Sometimes brand names, like Kleenex, are so well known that they become a synonym for the product or service. Want to know a song title? Just Shazam it!

In November 2013, Shazam partnered with Mindshare, which is also the name of a global marketing company. Shazam wanted to tie commercials to songs or sound effects. Brand name products could "buy" a song just as businesses bid for search terms on Google. Then someone uses Shazam to identify that particular song apart from a commercial. What happens? The advertiser who bought that song will be able to attach itself to that sound track. For example, suppose a potato chip company uses a particular song in its commercials and purchases the right to attach its product to that song. You might download that song—just because you love it—and along with the song comes an ad or coupon for that particular brand of potato chips. In addition to songs, catchy jingles can be made Shazamable, as well as sound effects (such as a pet food brand using the audio fingerprint of a barking dog).

Partnering with the marketing company Mindshare gives the Shazam company critical information about how people are using technology. This, in turn, helps shape Shazam's plans for the future. For example, research on MindshareWorld.com "explodes the myth that all consumers are smartphone-wielding, tablet-tapping technophiles accessing digital services on the move." The research found that people actually still preferred using laptops or desktop computers instead of smartphones and tablets.

This MindshareWorld.com study of forty-two thousand consumers from forty-two countries showed that more

Award-Winning Shazam

Shazam's successes have been recognized through numerous awards. The honor represented by the awards shows appreciation for a high-quality service and keen business success. Winning awards builds trust in the company, for both users and investors. Following is just a partial list of Shazam's awards:

- Sports Social Television Awards for the NBC Olympic broadcast
- Mobile Entertainment Award for Best Music Service Provider
- Best Management Team Award from the *Sunday Times* (United Kingdom) in its Tech Track 100 Awards
- CSI Award for Best Interactive TV Technology of Application
- Social Television Award (Steevee) for Best Branded Television
- The Mobile Marketing Association's Global and North American Industry Awards for Overall Excellence
- The Queen's Award for Enterprise and Innovation, one of the United Kingdom's most prestigious awards

- The Companion & Second Screen Prize at the Connected World Summit

than 90 percent of respondents used a laptop or desktop on a regular basis, compared to 56 percent who used a smartphone and just 33 percent who owned a tablet. Although the use of both smartphones and tablets is increasing, the majority of people are still using traditional technology to access the Internet. Users in the United States are still more likely to do online activities at home, using a laptop or desktop computer because the screen is bigger. So Shazam won't want to ignore these users as they develop new services. This kind of Mindshare marketing research is extremely valuable to Shazam.

"RADIO ON STEROIDS"

That's how Susan Lintonsmith, the chief marketing officer of Quiznos sandwich chain, described a new advertising test in November 2013. Imagine this. A Quiznos restaurant is a block away. As drivers in the vicinity listen to a song associated with the Quiznos brand, they hear a commercial promoting restaurant offers (like coupons) for Quiznos. The offers are also displayed on the car's touch screen.

Shazam is working with businesses like Quiznos to link songs with goods and services in a driver's vicinity. While listening to a song, coupons appear on the car's touch screen.

Touching a thumbs-up icon on the screen will send a coupon by e-mail that can be redeemed immediately at the store. The driver may not have intended to visit Quiznos—he may not even be hungry—but now he pulls into its parking lot. Drivers see this as "value added," not intrusive advertising.

The Quiznos test depended on a couple of different technologies to work. First, drivers needed to be listening to Aha Radio when they approached the Quiznos store. Aha Radio is an in-dashboard, easy-to-use interface that makes finding your music an easy process, like turning a radio dial. It helps you organize your favorites in pre-set, easy-to-find lists. An Aha-enabled stereo takes care of finding all your favorite listening content for you and delivering it through your stereo.

Second, the Quiznos store sending out the advertising needed to have a "geo-fence" around it so that when drivers crossed that line, they would hear a commercial for Quiznos. A geo-fence is a virtual border or boundary around a real physical area, like the store. A geo-fence can be small (around a single house) or larger (around an entire school attendance zone). Geo-fencing is a feature in a software program that uses the Global Positioning System (GPS) or radio frequency identification (RFID) to identify geographical boundaries.

By 2014, this was still in the testing stage, but as the innovations from Shazam keep rolling out, app users will undoubtedly begin seeing targeted marketing just like this.

IPO, OR GOING PUBLIC

Because of the money Shazam is now generating, there is growing speculation that it will soon become a publicly owned company when it decides to sell stock in the company (like Facebook did). An IPO (initial public offering) is the first sale of stock by a private company to the public who want to invest in this dynamite company. An IPO doesn't happen until there is sufficient public confidence in a company. Otherwise, the stock won't sell at a good price. Going public—and inspiring public confidence in the company's stock—requires solid financial growth.

The app marketplace has a reputation for being chaotic—lots of ups and downs. Here today, gone tomorrow. But Shazam has overcome that kind of reputation with regular improvements to its app capability. And by and large, the users themselves rave about the app and its many uses. For many years, Shazam has demonstrated consistent growth. Moving into areas like Smart TV and TV tagging has kept the app new and fresh.

Then in July 2013, a financial event occurred that grabbed attention around the world. Carlos Slim, a man that *Forbes* magazine named the "Richest Man in the World" from 2010 to 2013, invested a whopping $40 million in the company. Slim is confident that Shazam is the future of tech and search capability. He believes that Shazam still has the room and ability to grow.

So is a Shazam IPO just around the corner? Not quite yet. Something as big as taking a private company public can't be rushed. In an interview on TechWorld. com, executive chairman Andrew Fisher says an IPO could happen before 2020. The company wants to be as well known, widespread, and diversified as possible before making such a move. It has to be sure that the benefits of being a public company are great enough to make the change. In 2013, Rich Riley joined Shazam

Carlos Slim, dubbed the richest man in the world, grabbed worldwide attention when he invested $40 million in Shazam. That was a huge vote of confidence in Shazam's future.

as CEO after fourteen years at Yahoo! His task was to guide Shazam onto the stock market through the process of going public, also known as flotation. In an interview on FoxBusiness.com in January 2014, Riley agreed that Shazam was "at least twelve months away from an IPO."

When a company goes public, it must choose a market. Shazam's head office is in London, and most of its employees live there, but the company is open-minded about choosing Europe or North America. The government of the United

Kingdom and the London Stock Exchange have introduced some incentives in recent years designed to encourage British companies to list on London's stock markets and stay in the United Kingdom.

LOOKING TO THE FUTURE

Shazam is showing astonishing growth. It crossed the 350 million user mark and 80 million monthly active user mark in August 2013. By January 2014, Shazam was adding ten million users per month. There were 15 million Shazams, or tags, per day, which amounted to more than 3.5 billion tags a year. Shazam sold over five hundred thousand songs per day (over $300 million worth of songs per year). According to FinancialTimes.com, in January 2014, Shazam was one of the ten most popular iPhone apps downloaded worldwide.

Shazam helps sell products—and not just songs. It places ads within the apps where people spend more time (and where Shazam has a supply of product to sell). Shazam also sells through social media. Listeners don't just buy songs they have tagged themselves. Now they may simply see a song recommended by a friend on Facebook and buy it as a result.

Shazam wants to be the place where people go at any time, even when they aren't listening to music. They might go to Shazam to see what music their friends (or people around the world) are listening to. What does

Joining the Shazam Team

Want to work for Shazam? Phil Kench, the senior product manager, says the essence of Shazam's culture is being flexible. Shazam demands a lot from its team as it works in both music and television markets. The team must pull together to solve problems and build new features. There is good banter when the team is at work. With that work environment in mind, Kench says these three things make the ideal Shazam employee:

1. Quick to learn
2. Open to change
3. Experimenter

Shazam do with that information? Why does it care what you're listening to? Among other things, Shazam is now used by the music industry to accurately predict which new songs and artists will go to the top of the charts. The Shazam tag chart is seen by the music industry as a true indicator of interest in a particular track or artist. Because Shazam receives more than ten million tags each day, it notices which songs people find intriguing enough to tag for more information about the singer or band. This knowledge lets Shazam predict which songs will go on to become hits. It has had astounding accuracy. More than 85 percent of the songs that top the Shazam tag chart go on to lead the national charts.

And now users can auto-tag certain sounds, music, TV shows, and commercials in the background all day long. Shazam maintains a list of the things it has identified so that you can keep track of the songs you heard, for example, on the radio, on the way to work, or heading to school. Auto Shazam works even if the phone is locked or another app is being used. Some people worry about privacy though, and Shazam is sensitive to that. The automatic identification service is an opt-in system; you have to deliberately enable it in the app in order to use it.

At this point, you might be thinking what hundreds of app users are thinking—that you have a ground-breaking idea for an app to build yourself and make a fortune! There are many books on the market claiming to show you how. What advice would Chris Barton give you? As he states in *Mad Men of Mobile*, "My biggest piece of advice is to be careful about the assumption of 'If I build it, they will come.' In the mobile application ecosystem, 99 percent of mobile applications never get significant user adoption."

But if you do decide to take the plunge? In the same *Mad Men of Mobile* interview, Dhiraj Mukherjee

Can Shazam sustain its remarkable growth? Rich Riley, CEO of Shazam, thinks
so. Shazam will continue to blend important facets of its success: smartphones,
Internet, TV, and business.

advises strongly that you always stick to your values and not let them be "drowned out by inexperience, uncertainty, fear, greed, bad advice, or groupthink." He says it can be tempting to take shortcuts and let your standards slip. Don't do that.

There's no doubt about it: Shazam is a leader that is continually moving ahead. Can it sustain its remarkable growth? With all the innovative ideas it has developed in recent years, it appears that the Shazam team has every reason to be optimistic. As Rich Riley said in a RedHerring.com interview, "We are in a phase of accelerated growth . . . And we can anticipate that it will go faster in the near future." The best is yet to come!

CHRIS BARTON

Birthplace: United States

Education: BA from UC Berkeley, MBA from UC Berkeley, and a master's degree in finance from Cambridge University

Early Jobs: Eight years at Google, as well as jobs at Microsoft (MSN) and News Corp.

Current Residence: San Francisco

Current Job Title: Board member of Shazam and head of Mobile Carriers Business Development at Dropbox in San Francisco

Activities: Traveling, hiking

PHILIP INGHELBRECHT

Birthplace: Belgium

Education: BA from the University of Leuven, Belgium, and MBA from UC Berkeley

Early Jobs: Google (YouTube), founder of Road Hero, Inc.; president of TrueCar; and the inventor of the DriveMeCrazy app to report bad drivers

Current Residence: San Francisco

Current Job Title: Head of Business Development at RockMelt, Inc.

Activities: Kite-surfing, snowboarding, squash, swimming

DHIRAJ MUKHERJEE

Birthplace: Delhi, India

Education: BA from Dartmouth College and an MBA from Stanford Business School

Early Jobs: Digital engagement strategist for the SocialEdge team at Infosys, and senior strategist and project manager at Viant

Current Residence: London

Current Job Title: ?What If! Innovation Partner (Director)

Activities: Once backpacked around the world

AVERY WANG

Education: Graduate degrees in electrical engineering and mathematics from Stanford University, with a Ph.D. from Stanford on auditory source separation.

Current Residence: Bay Area, California

Current Job Title: Chief scientist at Shazam as well as chief author of its many patents (he has been there since 2000, with a brief interval away).

Fact Sheet on

SHAZAM

Founders: Chris Barton, Philip Inghelbrecht, Dhiraj Mukherjee, and Avery Wang

Original Name: 2580

Headquarters: Global headquarters in London and New York, plus offices in Menlo Park, California; Los Angeles, California; Chicago, Illinois; and Seoul, Korea.

Three Versions Offered: The free Shazam app (with advertising); Shazam Encore (no advertising, plus extra features); and Shazam RED (no advertising, plus part of the fee is donated to programs to fight HIV/AIDS in Africa)

Important Dates:

- 1999: Shazam starts up.

- 2000: Wang invents the audio recognition algorithm.

- 2002: The app is launched.

- 2000–2007: Shazam is primarily a dial-up service for mobile phones.

- 2005: Shazam puts mobile apps into use.

- 2008: Shazam launches as a featured iPhone app in the App Store.

- 2011: One hundred million people around the world have used Shazam.

- 2012: Shazam participates in its first Super Bowl event.

- 2013: Shazam lands $40 million from América Móvil to develop its TV ad business.

- 2013: TV tagging becomes available for U.S. TV stations.

2014 Shazam Statistics:

- More than 375 million Shazam app users around the world

- More than 75 million monthly active users

- Drove more than $300 million in digital goods sales between 2013 and 2014

- Available in 33 languages in more than 200 countries

- More than 10 million new fans added every month

- More than 15 million tracks, TV shows, and ads tagged, on average, each day

- More than 35 million audio tracks in the Shazam database

Timeline

1998: Chris Barton meets Philip Inghelbrecht in a business school class at UC Berkeley.

1999: Barton is hiking in the Himalayas when the idea for a music recognition app occurs to him.

Barton takes a class at the London Business School called Strategic Innovation; he re-establishes his friendship with Dhiraj Mukherjee, who is working in London.

Barton and Inghelbrecht have to choose one of their many ideas for a business, and they choose Shazam.

2000: Barton, Inghelbrecht, and Mukherjee meet Avery Wang in California. Wang agrees to be the fourth cofounder and later that year invents the audio recognition algorithm.

Shazam relocates to London; Wang then joins the other cofounders in London to help with fund-raising.

Shazam moves out of its first office (Mukherjee's apartment) and into its first real office at Wardour Street in the heart of the Soho district in London.

2000–2001: Shazam partners with Entertainment UK, the biggest wholesale distributor of CDs in the United Kingdom, to allow Shazam to build its database from its CDs. Twenty Shazam employees work 24/7 keying in the data from the songs.

Timeline (continued)

2000–2002: The cofounders work tirelessly to raise money from angel investors and venture capitalists. One million dollars is raised in angel funds and $4.5 million from venture capitalists.

2002: Shazam's first CEO, Jerry Roest, is hired.

August 19, 2002: Shazam is launched exactly on schedule as "2580," a dial-up music app.

2000–2007: Shazam is primarily a dial-up service on mobile phones. The cofounders continue to raise money from investors. Barton, Mukherjee, and Inghelbrecht each exit after different rounds of funding, while Wang remains as chief scientist.

2005: Shazam starts putting mobile apps into use in a limited way.

2008: Shazam is chosen as a featured iPhone app on the App Store, exploding the business.

2011: By this point, one hundred million people around the world have used Shazam.

2012: Shazam's first Super Bowl event is a huge success, and it is featured on *Britain's Got Talent* and the Grammy Awards.

April 2013: Rich Riley, a former Yahoo! executive, assumes the role of CEO to prepare Shazam to go public on the stock market.

May 2013: Shazam lands $40 million from América Móvil to develop its TV ad business and grow in Latin America.

Late 2013: TV tagging is available for U.S. TV stations.

May 2014: Warner, Universal, and Sony (the world's biggest record companies) buy stakes in Shazam.

Shazam predicts the ten songs that will rise to the charts during the summer of 2014. Because of past successful predictions, individual buyers and stores listen closely now to Shazam's predictions.

Glossary

Android Google's operating system designed to work on mobile devices, including smartphones, tablet PCs, and e-book readers.

angel investor A financially successful individual who invests his or her own personal funds into a new business that has potential.

app Application; a program usually designed for a specialized purpose that can be downloaded on smartphones and other mobile devices.

audio imprint An identifying characteristic of a song, much like a fingerprint helps identify people.

brand adoption rate How long it takes after hearing about a product or service before the public adopts it and uses it.

cofounder One person of a group of people who establish something together.

conversion rate A measurement of how many app users or website visitors are transformed into paying customers.

database A collection of information arranged for ease and speed of search and retrieval.

entrepreneur A person who organizes, operates, and assumes the risk for a business venture.

flotation The process of changing a private company into a public company by issuing shares for the public to purchase.

geo-fence An invisible virtual border or boundary around a real physical area.

innovative Using or creating new methods and ideas.

iPhone A line of Internet and multimedia-enabled smartphones designed and marketed by Apple.

IPO Initial public offering; the first sale of stock by a private company to the public.

launch The point at which a consumer first has access to a new product or service.

media engagement A person's involvement, participation, and interaction with various media sources.

middleman A trader who buys products from producers and acts as a go-between, selling the products to consumers.

mind share Consumer awareness or perception about a service or product, generally developed through marketing and advertising campaigns.

numeric signature Patterns of frequency within music that are as unique to a song as handwritten signatures.

patent A government license giving someone the sole right to make, use, or sell an invention.

per capita The average amount of anything per person.

platform An underlying computer system (such as iOS, Android, or BlackBerry) that allows applications to operate.

second screen A mobile device (such as a smartphone or tablet) used to enhance the experience of what is being watched on TV.

Silicon Valley An area south of San Francisco, California, that is noted for its large number of computer companies.

smartphone A cellular telephone with built-in applications and Internet access. It turns a cell phone into a sort of personal computer.

social network Online website, such as Facebook, Twitter, or Google+, where people can connect and share information with others.

spectrogram A visual representation on a graph of the range of frequencies in a particular sound.

start-up A business or operation that is just beginning.

tagging Using the Shazam app to identify and mark a song in order to get data about the song.

venture capitalist (VC) A person who invests a large amount of other people's money in a business endeavor, in exchange for significant control over company decisions and part ownership of the new company.

Canadian Advanced Technology Alliance (CATA)

207 Bank Street, Suite 416

Ottawa, ON K2P 2N2

Canada

(613) 236-6550

Website: http://www.cata.ca

The largest high-tech association in Canada, CATA is
a complete resource for the latest high-tech news
in Canada. CATA Alliance matches businesses with
opportunities across almost every region.

CTIA—The Wireless Association

1400 16th Street NW, Suite 600

Washington, DC 20036

Website: http://www.ctia.org

CTIA helps consumers use wireless technology
responsibly, through such campaigns as "On the
Road, Off the Phone," a teen-focused safe driving
public service program.

Digital Media Association (DiMA)

1050 17th Street NW

Suite 220

Washington, DC 20036

(202) 639-9509

Website: http://www.digmedia.org

DiMA promotes responsible use of new media such
as online music, books, and video content and
advocates for legal initiatives that nurture fair and
sustainable online business practices.

Don't Buy It: Get Media Smart

Public Broadcasting Service

2100 Crystal Drive

Arlington, VA 22202

Website: http://pbskids.org/dontbuyit

Don't Buy It: Get Media Smart is a website for young
people that encourages users to become smart consumers. Activities provide users with knowledge
needed to question and evaluate media messages.

Interactive Advertising Bureau (IAB)

116 East 27th Street, 7th Floor

New York, NY 10016

(212) 380-4700

Website: http://www.iab.net

IAB encourages companies to explore interactive
advertising and teaches professionals best practices
and the proper use of interactive advertising.

International Digital Media and Arts
　　Association (iDMAa)
P.O. Box 622
Agoura Hills, CA 91376-0622
Website: http://idmaa.org
(818) 564-7898
iDMAa is dedicated to serving educators, practitio-
　　ners, scholars, and organizations with interests in
　　digital media.

The Internet Society
1775 Wiehle Avenue, Suite 201
Reston, VA 20190
(703) 439-2120
Website: http://www.internetsociety.org
The Internet Society promotes the open development
　　and use of the Internet for the benefit of all people
　　throughout the world. Forums for discussion of tech-
　　nical, commercial, and societal issues are provided.

MediaSmarts
950 Gladstone Avenue, Suite 120
Ottawa, ON K1Y 3E6
Canada
(800) 896-3342
Website: http://www.mediasmarts.ca
MediaSmarts promotes education, public awareness,

and research in media literacy, especially among children and youth. Its research initiatives include "Young Canadians in a Wired World," which examines how to keep kids safe in a wired world.

One Economy Corporation
1776 I Street NW, 9th Floor
Washington, DC 20006
(202) 393-0051
Website: http://www.justthink.org
One Economy Corporation seeks to connect underserved communities around the world with technology. Its Just Think project is devoted to teaching young people to understand the words and images in media and to think for themselves.

OpenMedia
1424 Commercial Drive
P.O. Box 21674
Vancouver, BC V5L 5G3
Canada
(604) 633-2744
Website: http://www.openmedia.ca
OpenMedia helps safeguard an open and affordable Internet through citizen campaigns. OpenMedia has shown that the pro-Internet community can come together and make change.

Wired Safety
Contact form: https://www.wiredsafety.org/contact/
Website: http//www.wiredsafety.org
Wired Safety provides one-to-one help, extensive
    information, and education to cyberspace users
    of all ages. It includes the award-winning Tween
    Angels teen cyber safety expert group.

WEBSITES

Because of the changing nature of Internet links, Rosen
Publishing has developed an online list of websites
related to the subject of this book. This site is updated
regularly. Please use this link to access the list:

http://www.rosenlinks.com/IBIO/Shaz

For Further Reading

Beach, Jim, et al. *School for Startups: The Breakthrough Course for Guaranteeing Small Business Success in 90 Days or Less*. New York, NY: McGraw-Hill, 2011.

Berger, Jonah. *Contagious: Why Things Catch On*. New York, NY: Simon & Schuster, 2013.

Chidgey, Chris. *The Mobile Apps Fastlane—The Fast Track to Getting Started with Mobile App Development, Publishing and Creating a Mobile Apps Business*. San Francisco, CA: BGB Island LLC, 2013.

Dushinski, Kim. *The Mobile Marketing Handbook: A Step-by-Step Guide to Creating Dynamic Mobile Marketing Campaigns*. Medford, NJ: Information Today, Inc., 2012.

Erwin, Kim. *Communicating the New: Methods to Shape and Accelerate Innovation*. Hoboken, NJ: Wiley, 2013.

Gordon, Steve. *The Future of the Music Business: How to Succeed with the New Digital Technologies*. Milwaukee, WI: Hal Leonard, 2011.

Grant, August E., ed. *Communication Technology Update and Fundamentals*. Burlington, MA: Focal Press, 2012.

Gurrieri, Jordan, and Bobby Gill. *Appsters: A Beginner's*

Guide to App Entrepreneurship. New York, NY: Blue Label Labs, 2013.

Hopkins, Jeanne, and Jamie Turner. *Go Mobile: Location-Based Marketing, Apps, Mobile Optimized Ad Campaigns, 2D Codes and Other Mobile Strategies to Grow Your Business.* Hoboken, NJ: Wiley, 2012.

Johnson, Kevin. *The Entrepreneur Mind: 100 Essential Beliefs, Characteristics, and Habits of Elite Entrepreneurs.* Atlanta, GA: Johnson Media, 2013.

Keeley, Larry. *Ten Types of Innovation: The Discipline of Building Breakthroughs.* Hoboken, NJ: Wiley, 2013.

Klein, Jeff. *Mobile Marketing: Successful Strategies for Today's Mobile Economy: Put the Power of Mobile Apps, Mobile Websites, SMS and QR Codes to Work for Your Business.* Seattle, WA: Amazon.com CreateSpace Independent Publishing, 2013.

Krum, Cindy. *Mobile Marketing: Finding Your Customers No Matter Where They Are.* Indianapolis, IN: Que Publishing, 2010.

Kusek, David and Gerd Leonhard. *The Future of Music.* Boston, MA: Berklee Press, 2009.

Lee, Shane. *AppSource: Discover How 10 Successful iPhone App Entrepreneurs Hit It Big Outsourcing the Development of their Apps.* Beginning IOS Development (online only), 2014.

Livingston, Jessica. *Founders at Work: Stories of Startups' Early Days*. Berkeley, CA: APRESS, 2007.

Martin, Chuck. *Mobile Influence: The New Power of the Consumer*. Basingstoke, England: Palgrave Macmillan, 2013.

Martin, Chuck. *The Third Screen: Marketing to Your Customers in a World Gone Mobile*. Boston, MA: Nicholas Brealey, 2011.

Mui, Chunka, and Paul Bo Carroll. *The New Killer Apps: How Large Companies Can Out-Innovate Start-Ups*. Chicago, IL: Devils Advocate Group, 2013.

Mureta, Chad. *App Empire: Make Money, Have a Life, and Let Technology Work for You*. Hoboken, NJ: Wiley, 2012.

Napoli, Philip M. *Audience Evolution: New Technologies and the Transformation of Media Audiences*. New York, NY: Columbia University Press, 2010.

Rohrs, Jeffrey. *Audience: Marketing in the Age of Subscribers, Fans and Followers*. Hoboken, NJ: Wiley, 2012.

Rowles, Daniel. *Mobile Marketing: How Mobile Technology Is Revolutionizing Marketing, Communications and Advertising*. London, England: Kogan Page, 2013.

Saylor, Michael. *The Mobile Wave: How Mobile Intelligence Will Change Everything*. New York, NY: Vanguard Press, 2012.

Scott, David Meerman. *The New Rules of Marketing & PR: How to Use Social Media, Online Video, Mobile Applications, Blogs, News Releases, and Viral Marketing to Reach Buyers Directly*. Hoboken, NJ: Wiley, 2011.

Watkins, Michael. *The First 90 Days, Updated and Expanded: Proven Strategies for Getting Up to Speed Faster and Smarter*. Boston, MA: Harvard Business Review Press, 2013.

Wheeler, Alina. *Designing Brand Identity: An Essential Guide for the Whole Branding Team*. Hoboken, NJ: Wiley, 2012.

Bibliography

Bad App Reviews. "Bad App Reviews for Shazam."
April 9–April 23, 2012. Retrieved February 16, 2014
(http://www.badappreviews.com/iosapps/3383/
shazam/17).

Chacksfield, Marc. "The Evolution of Shazam: from Music
Maestro to TV Tagging." *Tech Radar*, September 22,
2013. Retrieved February 16, 2014 (http://www
.techradar.com/us/news/television/x-1182901).

Chaey, Christina. "Shazam Already Helps You Discover
Music, Now It Wants to Help You Discover TV
Advertising." *Fast Company*, September 17, 2012.
Retrieved February 15, 2014 (http://www.fastcompany.
com/3001331/shazam-already-helps-you-discover-
music-now-it-wants-help-you-discover-tv-advertising).

Common Sense Media. "What Parents and Kids Say."
August 2010–November 2013 reviews. Retrieved
February 16, 2014 (http://www.commonsensemedia.
org/app-reviews/shazam-encore).

Georger, Mary. "Shazam Founder Avery Wang on
Inspiration, Insights and Mobile Trends." The Recapp,
May 17, 2012. Retrieved February 16, 2014 (http://
www.therecapp.com/app_nation/5_questions/
shazam_founder_avery_wang_innovation_insights_
mobile_trends).

Horowitz, Ben. "How Angel Investing Is Different Than Venture Capital." *Business Insider*, March 2, 2010. Retrieved February 15, 2014 (http://www .businessinsider.com/how-angel-investing-is-different-than-venture-capital-2010-3).

HypeBot. "Shazam Finds More Ways to Increase Music Sales with Top Charts in Amazon's MP3 Store." Retrieved February 16, 2014 (http://www.hypebot.com/hypebot/2013/11/ shazam-finds-more-ways-to-increase-music-sales-with-top-charts-in-amazons-mp3-store.html).

Mills, Will. "Thirteen Years On and Shazam Is Still Magic." *Matterz*, February 1, 2013. Retrieved February 16, 2014 (http:// www.matterz.co.uk/news-reviews/ thirteen-years-on-and-shazam-is-still-magic).

MindShare. "On the Eve of CES New Research Reveals It's More Likely to Be the Place Not the Device That Matters Most If You Want to Get Your Messages Across to Consumers." January 3, 2014. Retrieved February 16, 2014 (http://www.mindshareworld.com/who-we-are /news/@places-not-platforms-research).

Newman, Danielle. *Mad Men of Mobile: Leading Entrepreneurs and Innovators Share Their Stories, from SIRI to SHAZAM*. Seattle, WA: CreateSpace Independent Publishing, 2013.

Reuters. "Shazam's Super Bowl Launch Party: Free Cars, Live Stats and Exclusive Music." February 2, 2012. Retrieved February 15, 2013. (http://www.reuters.com/article/2012/02/02/idUS372564113920120202).

Santos, Pedro Gairifo. *European Founders at Work*. New York, NY: Apress, 2012.

Schenker, Jennifer L. "Shazam's Saga: Scaling Up Has Its Perils and Its Rewards." Informilo, December 3, 2013. Retrieved February 16, 2014 (http://www.informilo.com/20131203/shazams-saga-scaling-has-its-perils-and-its-rewards-709).

Shead, Sam. "Shazam Reveals IPO Could be Two Years Away." *Tech World*, December 17, 2013. Retrieved February 15, 2014 (http://news.techworld.com/sme/3494171/shazam-reveals-ipo-could-be-two-years-away).

Sisario, Ben, and Stuart Elliott. "Shazam Deal Aims to Tie Songs Fast to Products." *New York Times*, November 24, 2013. Retrieved February 16, 2014 (http://www.nytimes.com/2013/11/25/business/media/an-attempt-to-tie-a-song-fast-to-a-product.html?smid=tw-nytimesmusic&seid=auto&_r=1&#h[AiaAwy,2]).

Slash Gear. "Shazam Adds Auto-Tagging: Always Listening to Your Music and TV." May 23, 2013.

Retrieved February 16, 2014 (http://www.slashgear.
com/shazam-adds-auto-tagging-always-listening-to-
your-music-and-tv-23283319).

Social Safety Patrol. "Shazam for Redband Trailers."
April 24, 2013. Retrieved February 16, 2014 (http://
thesocialsheriff.wordpress.com/2013/04/24/shazam
-for-redband-trailers/?relatedposts_exclude=1811).

Tripathi, Shruti. "Can Shazam Be UK's First Billion-Dollar
Tech Company?" London Loves Business, February
27, 2013. Retrieved February 16, 2014 (http://www.
londonlovesbusiness.com/entrepreneurs/famous-
entrepreneurs/can-shazam-be-uks-first
-billion-dollar-tech-company/4845.article).

Walker, Daniela. "Music Identification App Expands Its
Capabilities to Fashion Finding." PSFK, April 8, 2013.
Retrieved February 16, 2014 (http://www.psfk
.com/2013/04/shazam-clothing-identification
-tv-shows.html#!v1ZC8).

Wang, Avery Li-Chun. "An Industrial-Strength Audio Search
Algorithm." Shazam Entertainment, Ltd. Retrieved
February 16, 2014 (http://www.ee.columbia.edu/~dpwe
/papers/Wang03-shazam.pdf).

Index

V

W

Y

ABOUT THE AUTHOR

Kristi Holl is the author of forty-two published books. She bought one of the earliest computers—a KayPro II the size of a suitcase—and thought writing on the green screen was magical. Later the Internet came along, making research a breeze. Then, with smartphones and social networking, it was no longer lonely being a writer. While she has never invented an app, she appreciates how Shazam's innovations have raised the world's media experience to a whole new level.

PHOTO CREDITS

Cover, pp. 3, 7, 99 Bloomberg/Getty Images; pp. 11, 46 © Camera Press/ Jonathan Player/Redux; p. 13 Jan Haas/DPA/Landov; p. 15 Hulton Archive/Getty Images; p. 17 DJ40/Shutterstock.com; p. 25 © iStockphoto .com/Erik Khalitov; p. 27 © iStockphoto.com/Cottonfioc; p. 29 Gary S Chapman/Photographer's Choice/Getty Images; p. 31 Science Source; p. 36 Telekhovskyi/Shutterstock.com; p. 41 Science & Society Picture Library/Getty Images; p. 44 Marques/Shutterstock.com; p. 48 Kamira/ Shutterstock.com; p. 53 eurobanks/Shutterstock.com; p. 57 Dave Buresh/ Denver Post/Getty Images; p. 62 Monkey Business Images/Shutterstock .com; p. 66 sturti/E+/Getty Images; p. 71 Mehmet Dilsiz/Shutterstock .com; p. 73 Annette Shaff/Shutterstock.com; p. 75 Daniel Bockwoldt/ picture-alliance/dpa/AP Images; p. 81 Gregory Shamus/Getty Images; p. 84 Matt Sayles/Invision/AP Images; p. 86 Leontura/E+/Getty Images; pp. 88, 95 AP Images; p. 92 Kathryn Scott Osler/Denver Post/Getty Images; cover and interior pages background image dpaint/Shutterstock.com; pp. 20–21, 33, 50–51, 64, 79, 82, 90–91, 97 inset background image kentoh/ Shutterstock.com.

Designer: Brian Garvey; Editor: Shalini Saxena; Photo Researcher: Marty Levick